LETTERS TO GOYA

LETTERS TO GOYA
POEMS, TITLES AND LETTERS TO THE DEAD

JAMES MAGEE

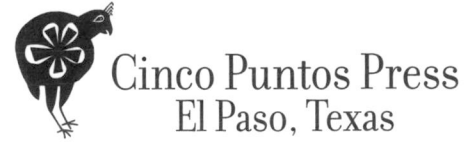
Cinco Puntos Press
El Paso, Texas

FIRST EDITION

1

Library of Congress Cataloging-in-Publication Data

Names: Magee, James R., author.
Title: Letters to Goya : poems, titles and letters to the dead / by James
   Magee.
Description: El Paso, Texas : Cinco Puntos Press, [2018]
Identifiers: LCCN 2018027163 | ISBN 978-1-941026-98-4 (pbk. : alk.
paper)
Classification: LCC PS3613.A34274 A6 2018 | DDC 811/.6—dc23
LC record available at https://lccn.loc.gov/2018027163

This book is set in Mrs. Eaves, designed in 1996 by Zuzana Licko. It was styled after Baskerville, a beloved transitional serif typeface designed in 1757 by John Baskerville in Birmingham, England. Mrs Eaves was named after Baskerville's live-in housekeeper, Sarah Eaves, whom he later married.

Cover: Annabel Livermore, *Chillicothe Lady*, oil on panel, 2016.
Design: Anne M. Giangiulio

❧

Thanks to Jill Bell for her work on both *Letters to Goya* and *Titles*. Thanks also to JB Bryan for his beautiful work on an earlier version of *Letters to Goya*.

IN MEMORY OF MY FATHER

❧

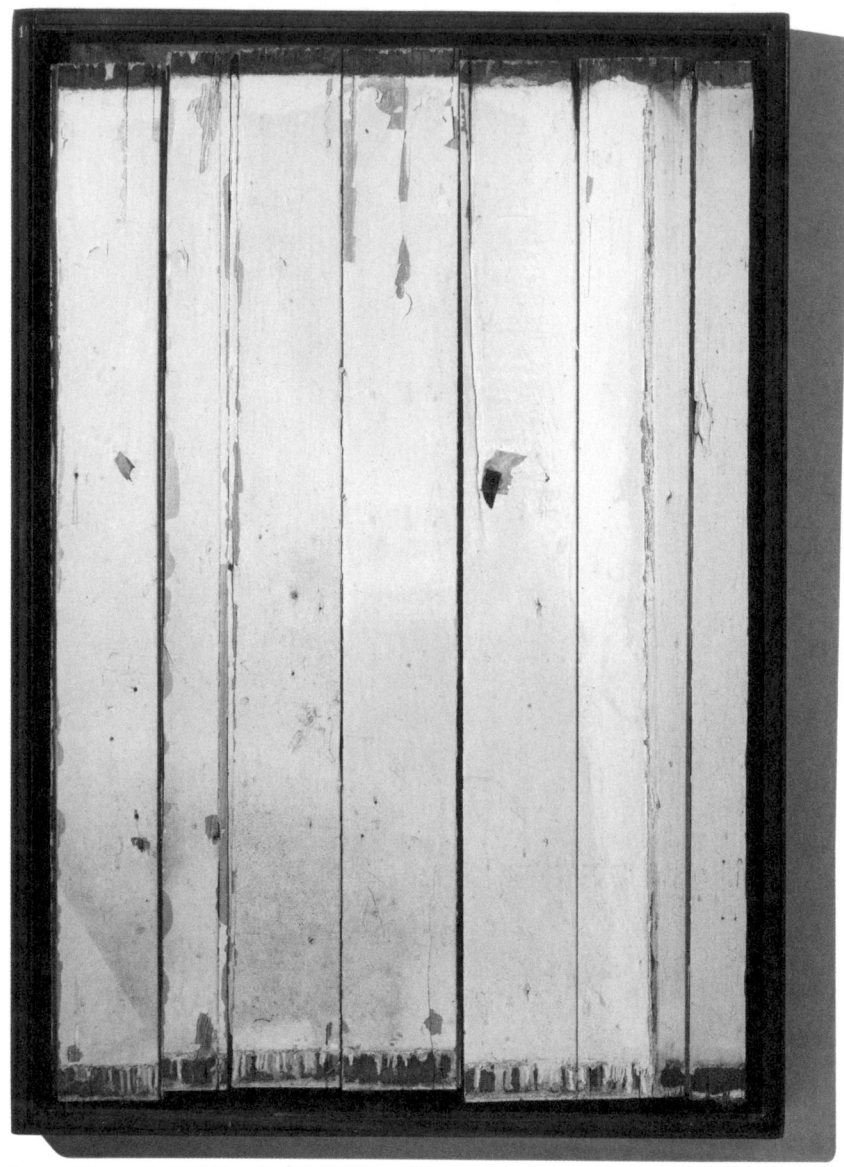

James Magee, *La Maja Desnuda [Duchess of Alba]*, mixed media,
51 5/8 x 35 ¾ inches, 1989.

Magee bought his workshop/warehouse on Myrtle Street in El Paso, Texas, in 1985, a huge space to create very large projects. In one corner of the workshop was a tiny and very dirty bathroom, and these boards were its wall. On the third wallboard from the right, about eye level if you are using the toilet, some worker had scratched a bit of graffiti (see facing page). Magee was intrigued by this little bit of graffiti. It reminded him almost magically of Goya's paintings of The Duchess of Alba, especially the one *La Maja Desnuda* (1797-1800), as reproduced in the "MiddleWord." The Duchess had been Goya's patron, and they may have been lovers, no one knows for sure. Many stories swirl around about their affair. But whatever the connection, Magee was inspired. He ripped the boards from the structural 2x4s and framed them in steel and glass. This became *La Maja Desnuda [Duchess of Alba]*, one of his assemblages.

A number of years after he had created the assemblage, on impulse Magee traveled to Sweetwater, Texas. He had had a good friend from his roughneck days in the Texas oilfields who was from Sweetwater, a dusty Texas town on the way to Dallas that carried a special sort of charm for Magee. The purpose of his journey was somehow to create a "title" for his porno assemblage. Jim got a cheap motel room and spent three or four days taking notes from *The Sweetwater Reporter* microfiche from 1955. From his research, he created the early 19th century Duchess who lived, oddly enough, in Sweetwater's Waikiki Trailer Park. This Duchess finger-pecked these strangely beautiful letters to her love interest Frankie Goya, Court Painter to His Majesty, Charles IV of Spain.

Her letters to Frankie became, in effect, the "Title" for Magee's *La Maja Desnuda [Duchess of Alba]*, pictured above. It all made perfect sense to James Magee. And it still does.

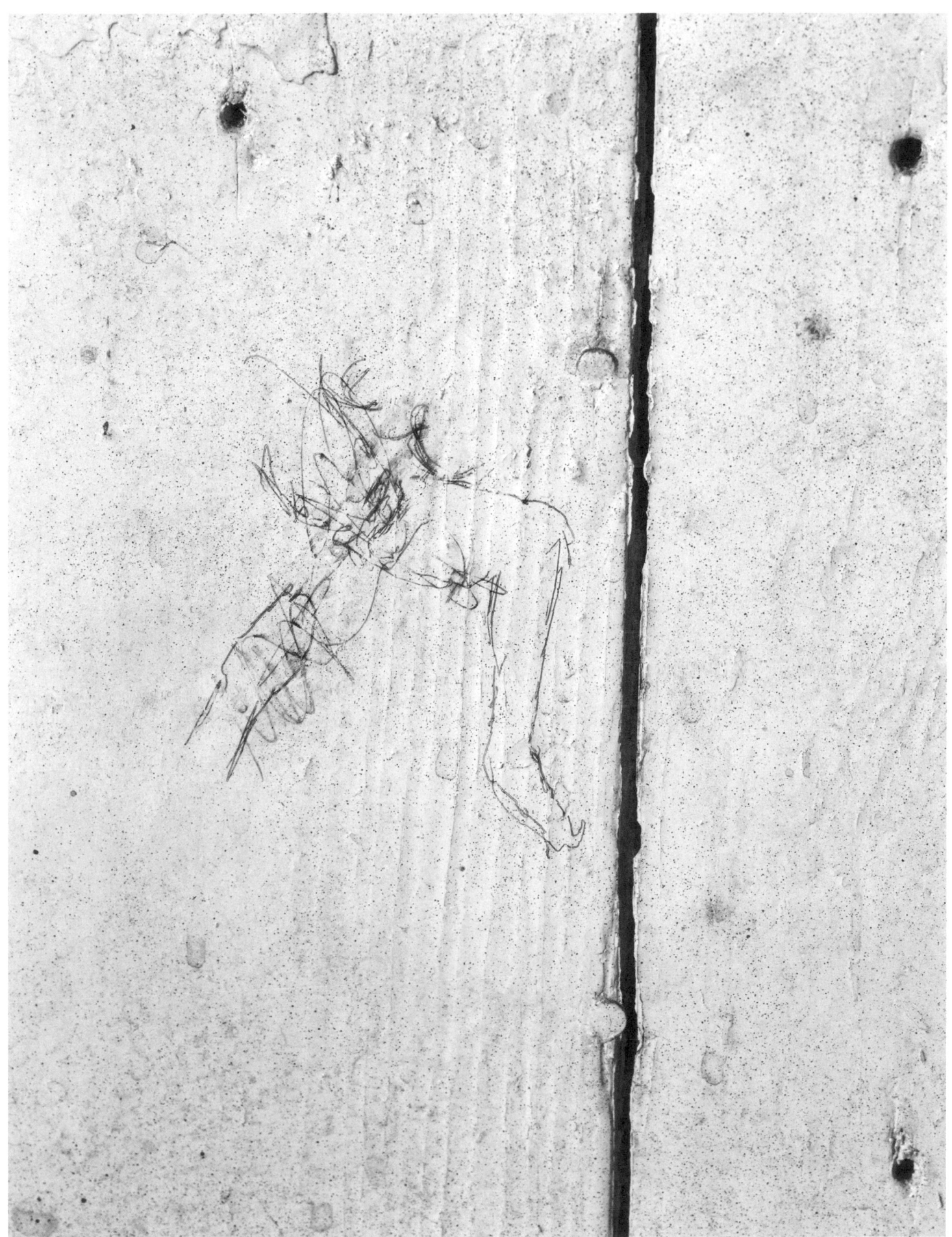

James Magee, detail of *La Maja Desnuda [Duchess of Alba]*, 1989.

❧

The following letters, dated
April 5th through September 15th, 1955,
from the Waikiki Trailer Park, Sweetwater, Texas,
were written by
Doña Maria del Pilar Teresa Cayetana de Silva Alvarez de Toledo,
13th Duchess of Alba
to
Francisco Jose de Goya y Lucientes,
Court Painter to His Majesty, Charles IV of Spain.

❧

LETTERS I–XXIII

James R. Magee : El Paso

April 5, 1955

Oh, Solo Goya,

                    has
    Can you believe it! Sears bath mats on sale for a dollar a mat and
I am standing here, like a damn fool, trying to figure out whether I
should rush down there before they8re all b̸o̸u̸t̸h̸d̸/ bought up.

    So indecisive. I keep thinking back on you lecturing me how no man,
having put his hand to the plough, and turning back, is fit for the
kingdom of God. But then again, maybe I am already in the kingdom right
here at the Wikiki. It¢s unfair to expect t everyone to be as self-assured
$̸ø̸ $̸ø̸ as you. I think clarity is a matter of grace, like strenghh, given
                                                          y
forth from the earth from which you were born; and Lord knows, and I donts̸a
His Name in vain, the earth arond Fuendetodos is plenty hard enough for my
chiny-chin-chin.

    Your darling,

The Duchess

/ April 11,1955

Dear Goya,

W.E. Wilkinson died yesterday from a stroke. It is a passing. For so many years I use to buy my b vegetables from him, when he had his store at 10th and Elm. Hearing about his death has not help/ helped my headaches, I suppose. And so this morning I went down to Ek's Garage to ask Ek about what he does when his headaches g get too rough.

Ek told me he uses an aire hose, the one next to h is tire rack. He just sticks it into his ear and lets it blow at 90 psi for 30 seconds or so. At first the blast of cold air kind of hurts real/bad, but then there comes an after shock which really picks up./ Ek says I'm not the first customer to tr y it out.

Tonight I rigged up an aire compressor to my alarm clock, which in turn is connected to an aire hose,which in turn I'm going to insert into my ear before I go to bed tonight. Ek says its a great way to wa wake up in the morning,

Yours, as always,

The Duchess

April 13, 1955

Dear Frank,

An old schoolmate of mine,who I havent seen in decades, called
me up out of the blue the other day. All I could remember about her
is that she peed in my bed when we were little girls, and now
to think she is about to become a grandmother for the fourth time.

Ida said her mother was sick and was going to die. I responeded
by telling her not to worry about her mother, that it was probably ¥¢
too late, qanyway, and that she might as well suck on lemons than to
shed tea rs. Besides, these scientist, not to mention the Almighty,
keep coming up with new medicines everyday, and who knows, maybe they
'll have something for old Mrs. Barlett, who 1 only remember from
the waist down, Frankie, cause she was so tall/ and big boned.

Have you heaa rd what they have now, speaking of all that?
Theyre coming out with a ¢¢¢/ vaccine for polio and they plan to give
all the first and second gradess two ¢h/¢¥// shots of the stuff
before the summer¢s over. Well, I need to go water the geraniums.

        Love,

    The Duchess (sigh)

April 19,1955

Dear Francisco,

   Lately I8ve been feeling sad and I cant put my finger on it. Maybe
it's because Bethy is moving awa y or that I feel I'm wasting my time
watching too much baseball on tvTV and not being attentive enough to
Bethy, whose moving back to Dallas to be closer to her mother, now that
Daryl8s gone and she has a little baby.

   Please, I must **talk** about these things. Maybe that's why I write to
you so much. I need to think there is someone out there listening and
just confessing that to you, even thog/ though you havent replied in a
long time, seems to lift a sdnss/ sadness from my breasts.

   At times like this Ifeel I've blown it, my likf/ life, I mean,
but what did I expect, anyway, Frankie? What did anyone expect? I was
given so much. Maybe looking back too much. Yet what did I do with it?
Just
   talked and looked at people wondering in and out of rooms, sitting
on my duff; and now that Bethy is about to lea ve, and she's been so
sweat to me, and to everyone, I dont know how to say goodbye to her.

   Wishing you were here,

        The Duchess

May 2nd, 1955

Dear Frank,

I barely dragged myself out of bed this morning. I had one of those mixer-upper drea-ms where everything is bent out of shape and you think you're in one city, when really you're standing on a corner street in another soliciting cheap favors from the passerbys. I felt like a regular whore, I mean in my sleep, and when I wokeup I just layed there in bed wondering what in God¢s name puts a dream like that into my head.

Which brings to me to Ruth Millet. You know how she gets under my sking; but sometimes, I admitm she makes sense, like the other day when she wrote in her colum that you must la-y the founda tion now if you want to become a gracious lady in yea rs ahead, like you should th think of others, be interested in their welfare, do little things to make them happy. But truth is, Goya, I probably think too much about myself, and now I'm wondering whether I should go to Galvestan for Splash Day Weekend, even though I've alrea dy bought me a new tanksuit and brea ch slippers. I suppose I could wear them around here in the yard. But they're scheduling a beauty contest over there on Saturday. Then Again, Frankie, what does beauty have to do with it ?

OOXX

The Duchess

May 10, 1955

Dear Goya,

Thank God we got rain yesterday and the day before. I was begining
to think we were all going to dry up and blow away. The storm hit Big ∅
Springs real hard, or that¢s what Mary Landford to∄d me. She also said she
gota call from her cou∄in, Henry, out in L.A., who I met some time ago
when he paid her a visit.

Anyway, to get to the point, Henry is dying and wants to be cremated
and he asked Mary to climb up theqBig Spring water tower to spread his
a-shes over the city at sunset. Well, Frank, last night Mary was all ∉∉∄∄
tears; and her husband thought Henry, whether he was dying or not,
was out of line, what with Mary8s arthritus and the prospect of her
trying to the climb to the top of the water tower at dusk. Besides, he
said, dying was her cousin8s business, not hers, and that Henry should n't
be so damn ∅∅¢/ operat∄cabout it.

I didnt know what to say. I cant think straight when someone, like,
Mary, is sobbing into the telephone. But what I **dent** understand is
why Henry, since he¢s been to Texas only once, is so set on being
spread all over Big Springs, though it is a pretty party of the country,
I admit.

I tried to talk Mary to drive over to Sweetwater tomarrow
night. I thought it would help ∄∄/∉∅∄∉ go with me to the midget
∉∉∉∉∉ wrestling match at the Armory. I think some of those little
cridders are kind of cute. But I doht think she's coming.

Any, way, I miss ∉ you

Lowing you,

The Duchess

May 18, 1955

Dear Francisco,

    Boy, was I down on my knees last night praying to Jesus.
A tornado almost hit Sweetwater. Im not sure if it has anything to
do with all this flying ¢¢¢¢/ saucer talk or the rains weve been
having lately.

    But you know I still pray after all these years and I say
grace before every meal. Even when Im in a restaarant I look down
at my plate and say I AM SORRY. Just think of it, Frank, that
hamberg er with catsup, mustar and pickles was only a short time
before walking around a field drinking out of a water hole, looking
for ward to a sunrise the next day and myabe nursing a calf.
How knows, maybe someday I'll be a piece of grizzle stuck between
two slices of bread looking up into your big brown y eyes, hoping
you'll gobble me right up.

    Lots of Hug and Kisses,

    The Duchess

May 22, 1955

Dear, Dear Frank,

        Jesus, how the young seem lost. Poor George, who lives with
his parents right next to me, and who just dropped out of school,
came stumbling through my door la6st night, his flesh more torn
than before----poor, ~~ppppr~~/ poor George: first it was a knife wound
to his chest, thanks to stepdad, then a broken wrist from falling off
                    then
the libra~~a~~ry roof, there were bruises to his cheek he tried to cover
up with mascara so that now I can barely distinguish him from that
        up
smashed fender on the side of my car. And yet, I tell you Goya, George
is more beautiful than ~~child~~/ any child I have seen sleeping under a
tree, and that's where he is right now infront of his family's trailer.
                                                        an
        But come to think of it, Frankie, you werent exactly angel,either
what with you and Mario stabbing that kid in Barcelona, then running off
to Madrid with Marsha Hunter. Boy, she sure thought she was something,
didnt she, with you on her arm and a Carrier 105 Delux aire
conditioner stra~~a~~pped to the side of her head. Oh well. ~~WHH~~/ How does
it go? Love, Forgiveness & Underst6anding,

        Sincerly, as always,

        The Duchess

June 5, 1955

Dear Frank,

    It seems yesterday was just "one of those days". I mean I had
a depression I couldnt shake. And This morning I woke up ~~i/t~~// feeling
                                            into
like ~~a/grey/a~~// a steel grey bird had flown up my nose and I couldnt
blow it out.

    Oh, la forca del destino. Oh, solo mio...to fall into your arms
again, Goya, how that would calm my nerves or to suck on your pretty
blue before walking down to the A & P to pick up a ~~pink~~/ pint of milk
for kitty.

       OOXXOOXXOOXXOOXXOOXXOOXXOOXXOOXX

The Duchess

June 17, 1955

Dear Frank,

Sometimes I look out my kitchen window and see Mr. Zurtlin
sitting in in my lawn chair. He doesnt say much. He teaches English
at the high sch ool. Mr. Zurtlin is what you'd call a deep thinker.
One of these days I am going to get up the coura ge to invite him in
                                          it
for a cup of coffee. I would have done this morning, but when I looked
outt the window a second time he was already gone.^I think he lives
at the Earle Hotel.

    Love,

    The Duchess

June 23, 1955

Dear Fra nk,

It seems everywhere you turn you meet people who think they're big shoots. Whey, I read today that that Duke of Edinburgh thought he could just plop his hilicopter right down in the middle of a football field to scare everyone, just because he's such a big deal.

It isnt ri̶g̶h̶t̶ right, Goya. But living in castles does tha to you. Think of that ding bat, dear Marie Luisa, thinking just because she¢s a queenybun, she c̶o̶u̶l̶ could steel that cute Don Juan Pignatelli from yours truly, and I was his step sister to ¢ begin with. The nerve.

Well, It¢s getting late. Lites out. Talk to you l̶a̶t̶¢ tomarrow mmaybe.

XX OO

The Duchess

July 3, 1955

Dear Goya,

    Today I ~~loaded my~~ loaded up the Chevy with my gear for a

a fishing trip on the Brazos, but blew a gasket 8 miles out of town.
So I guess I'll spend the fourth here in Sweetwater.

    Thinking of you on this h-oliday.

    Love,

The Duchess

July 5, 1955

Dear Goya,

Im ~~If~~ thinking about going down to the Sky Room tonight at the Blue Bonnett Hotel. Theyre putting on a ~~chik~~ chicken dinner for the 44 Dale Ca rnigie grads and Evelyn, who¢s trying to improve herself, will be receiving her dipolma. The only problem is the ~~Bule~~ **Sky** Room still has no carpet on the floor and the floor is filled with **cracks**, and I mean those **cracks** that seperate the planks of wood.

Well, you know Frankie ~~h//h/o//~~ how I hate **cracks** of anykind. Step on a crack and break your mother's back. Last time I was in the **Sky Room** I couldnt even walk across the floor to our dinner table. I just stood there. Frozen. With everyone in the d inning room egging me on. I felt like a fool. But I coulnt move.

It¢s even worse outside the A&P. I wish they would repair that side walk. Last Saturday it took me over fifteen minutes to walk just from the bus stop to ~~front//~~ the front entrance of the store, the concrete was so fractured; and when I left, an hour½ later, with two bags of groceries in my arms, it took me even longer.

Thinking of you,

The Duchess ☹

July 19,1955

Dear Frank,

The other day Lester Freeman, who lives two trailers away, connected the hot water line t o the bathroom shower, and it sure makes a difference. I can not only take hot showers now, but real steam baths as/as wwell. Let the hot water run on and on and soon th/ my entire trailer is filled with mist.

Now Lester and Bee come over in the afternoons and we all sit around with a six pack of beer and watch TV in our bathing suits.

Wish you were here.

Love,

The Duchess

July 28, 1955

/Dear Frank,

That Ruth Millet burns my top. Today she wrote in her
colum that even if youre smarter than your husband dont offer
him any advice. "Learn to relax and enjoy letting him him lead",
she says.
Well, that¢s what I tried to do with¢¢¢¢¢¢/ Don Jose, the
Dolt. Why did I ever marry him, anyway? Because I was young and
he
stupid and happened to be the 11th Marqui of Villafranca. ¢ Oh,
the glorious, so temorous and sensitive, slack jawed Jose Avarez
¢¢/¢¢¢¢¢¢/¢¢/// de Toledo Osorio Perez de Guzman, early-to-bed-
late-to-rise, couldnt get him off his fat ass even if Napolean
was blasting away at our front door.

Jesus, I think of the fool things I¢ve dome in my life....Cant
trust men, really. I even heard that Clark Gable had been cheating
on his former wife before he married that floosy, Kay Williams;
so you better not be cheating on me, Frankie.

Loving you in trust,

The Duchess

July 29, 1955

Dear Francisco,

It8s hard, but after all these years I still hurt from Isidro having ca lled me a witch. OK, maybe I'm too sensitive. But I bet that gardner of yours called other names, too. Tell me, who deserves that kind of abuse? / A Witxh! Well, I was always nice to him, wasn8t I, Frank?

Guess I0d/I'm feeeling0d bad about the World in general. The Yankees have fallen into second place and yesterday our Sweetwater P0n/ z Ponies lost to Snyder 5 to 2, and that's afer having beaten the pants off of Abilene the day before.

Love,

The Duchess

August 8, 1955

Dear Goya,

Holy molly, how Evylyn was in a tizzy. She calls me up
completely undone about how these sex f̷i̷n̷/ fiends raped and
murdered this kansas City socialite, and the lady, Evlyn says, was
only 34 years old.

Tell me, how are you suppose to respond? Ive never been to
Kansas City. I dont know what people do up there. So to calm her
down I suggest to Evlyn we go to a movie tonight. So I guess we're
going to catch the early show at the Rocket Drive-In. I t̷h̷i̷n̷k̷s̷///
think its a double with Brando in the <u>Wild One</u> and Merle
Oberon in B̷e̷r̷l̷i̷n̷/̷E̷x̷p̷r̷e̷s̷s̷// <u>Berlin Express</u>.

Wish you could join us,

The Duchess

August 16,1955

Dear Frank!

Guess What? ! The Yankees beat Baltimore six straight and
                        A couple of weeks ago
now theyre numero uno. Casey said they could win the penant

b and,by George, I think, Frank, he was right. Mantle just

has to keep hitting those homers. And Whitey has to keep striking

them out.   Club

Meanwhile, Evelyn is dead set on dragging me to the Garden

meeting tomarrow to help plan for the fall flower show. How

can I get out of that without hurting her feelings? There

theme will be " Flowers in Focus". Good Lord.

Love,

The Duchess

August 23, 1955

Dear Frqnk,

Thismorning I watered and repotted the geraniums l have
near the b¢¢k/ back door of the trailer. I really dont believe
in much beyond the sunlight shining down on my ¢¢ geraniums
and me. And I think that light is what churchpeople call kindness.

Love,

The Duchess

August 24, 1955

Dear Frank,

How many dresses can a woman wear at one time? Well, this lady can wear three: a pretty red and white one over a solid blue one under a pink and purple pokadot one out of Gachen¢s Dress Shoppe today. I dont think anyone saw me.

Thinking of ya,

The Duchess

September 3, 1955

Dear Francisco,

 Evlyn invited me over for dinner last night. The Martins
Were there, too. We had salad and tuna fish sandwiches, and after
the main course Evlyn, she¢s such a dear, ser~ed usblueberry ice
cream.

 Well, I got to talking again about rejoicing. How important
/1¥/1ø//1¥/1ø/it is to your soul to never forget. Its just that
some times I cant believe how beautiful ⱨøⱨ/ the world is. I get
so excited smelling freshly cut grass or taking my shoes off after
a thunderstorm, like we had a couple of nights ago, and going
barefoot around the trailer. It sends me soaring, if only for a few
moments. And when Im in that state, Frank, I begin to kiss everything
thing in sight, like I kiss my armˢ, my feet, the chair Im sitting
in, even the refrigerater door.

 Well, last night I kissed Mr. Martin. I dont know what came
over me. Evlyn tried to explain to Mrs. Martin I was in a state of
estasy. But it didnt seem to help matters. Actually, I dont
remember much. I must have been too close to his face. Anyway,
the Martins left without finishing their dessert.

Hoping youre doing well,

The Duchess

September 12, 1955

Dear Goya,

Oh, deary, I woke up this morning knowing Ezekiel had yelled
from a hilltop that the railroad tracks south of Broadway divide
the goats ffrom the sheep. I/c/d/ cant shake his voice out of my
head. It feels likeabucket of water.

Why repeat? repeat? repeat? I know every shred of life foretells
the future, like the way the wallpaper is peeling from my bedroom
ceiling is a sign, if only I could figure it out, or like those two
fat white woman running from their motel yelling for their children.

During times like these, when the sky opens up a crack and a
beam of light shines down upon the Lord's Prayer at our Garden of
Memories, I know Ezekiel is gallopping towards me on a fiery dapple
with flames b/l/o/ blowing out from his mouth. My /h/a/d/s/ hands tremble somuch
I cant even drink my morning coffee, like right now, if /y/o/u/r/ you
were sitting next to me, I¢d twist your nose right off, cutie.

Abundle of kisses,

The Duchess

September I5, I955

Dear Frank,

    Don𝙔 you yhink
    Dony you Y
    Dont You Think this world would be a better place if we all stopped

yacking for a moment and jsust kissed some one, I mean anyone, like say
the gas station man, what's his name, Sammy Furder. I know he works hard.

I'm sure he could use a kiss.

    Everyone talks and talks, and soon we start arguing and then we begin

to yell, and one thing leads to another and next thing you know the Israili'
and
    Egyptians are bashing each others heads and the Greeks and the Turks are

shooting it out over a piece of silly rock stuck somewhere in the oceqn, or

Arther Godrey, like a madman, is flyinghis by-plane into an airliner,

laughing that he was just jdipping his wing in salute, ha, ha, ha.

    Well, to get back to my point, today while I was down at Jane¢s

getting my hair fixed I saw the c sweetest little picture ø𝙛/ in a

magazine of little prince charlesstrutting behind his mom, Her Royal

H𝙄ghness, on their yaht, can you believe it, The Britannia, as they were lan
ing
    landing in Aberdeen, I just wanted to bend down and kiss his cute

little ears and pinch those pink English cheeks. I 𝙗𝙚𝙡𝙡/ tell you, Frankie,

some people really have it made.

    Sending more love than you can imagine,

        The Duchess

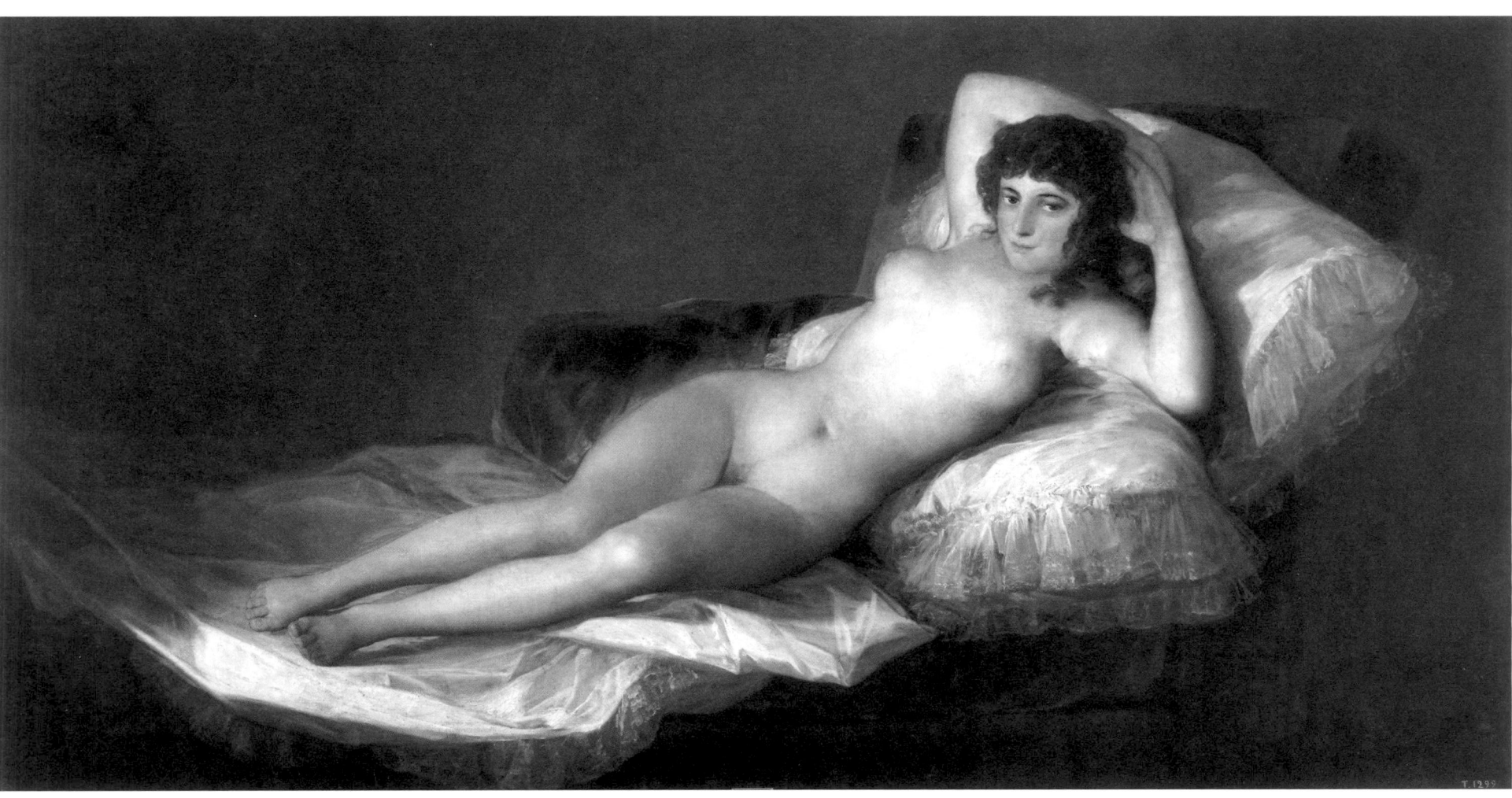

Francisco Goya, *La Maja Desnuda*, oil on canvas, c. 1797–1800.

MIDDLEWORD

BY KERRY DOYLE

"It is you talking as much as myself. I act as the tongue of you."
—*Walt Whitman*

❧

*"I got to talking again about rejoicing. About how important it is to your soul to never forget.
It's just that sometimes I can't believe how beautiful the world is."*
—*The Duchess*

❧

"I've been slithering around on this wet ground on all fours for so long now."
—*James Magee*

The words contained in this small surprising book are a window into the life of James Magee. Or perhaps they are many windows, some that look into mirrors, others that lead out to open doors. His has been a long life—and a complicated one. The more you get to know Jim, the more you understand that his life will never be visible from a single vantage point. Those people who know Jim well, and even some who don't, are aware that Jim has several alter-egos, perhaps somewhat less pathological than a split personality but more complicated and complex than a durational performance. There is Annabel Livermore, a retired librarian from the Midwest who took up painting later in life to great success and whose work has been exhibited in museums across the United States and collected by both individuals and institutions. Horace Mayfield has had a more modest career but, like Livermore and Magee, maintains his own independent residence and studio in El Paso, Texas. In the poems contained here we can see that the practice of channeling real or imagined others is central to Jim's being in the world. It is a kind of incarnate spirit that is embodied and expressed through a myriad of forms.

This book presents two bodies of writing by James Magee. The first is *Letters to Goya*, a collection of twenty-three typo-filled letters written on a manual typewriter from the Waikiki Trailer Park in Sweetwater, Texas. Turning the book around, you will find a second collection, a selected compilation of titles from Jim's artwork, representing decades of both writing and performance by the artist and his multiple selves. Reading this book is not unlike the act of trying to understand Jim's life. It requires twisting, turning, reorienting. You can enter at any point and find the story changing and growing as Jim plays conductor to a symphony of voices familiar and strange.

There is much that has been written in the last half century about the use of text by contemporary artists, but Jim's use of text is unique. The titles contained here (even *Letters to Goya* is a kind of title, written in homage to a simple pencil drawing on a bathroom wall) stand as separate literary works, and, for those lucky enough to experience them read by the artist in person, as performance pieces, something between channeling voices and spoken word poetry. The words that are included in this volume hint at the way that Jim exists in the world, equally attentive of small mysteries and terrible wonders. It is a kind of poetry that is highly evocative of the everyday, a streetwise *Song of Myself* in which Jim moves fluidly from voices that are both deeply distinctive and unmistakably universal. Though some art historians have been unable to resist speaking about Jim's art in religious or spiritual terms, the artist himself has lived a life very close to the ground. In his writing he takes us down there with him, a place far away from heaven but with a clear view of the sky.

At the beginning of *Letters to Goya*, Jim tells us that the letters have been written from the Waikiki trailer park in Sweetwater, Texas by Doña Maria del Pilar Teresa Cayetana de Silva Alvarez de Toledo, 13th Duchess of Alba to Francisco Jose de Goya y Lucientes, Court Painter to His Majesty, Charles IV of Spain. The original version of these letters was produced by the artist in 1995 on a manual typewriter, and the yellowed pages show the layered embossing left by metal keys as the duchess strikes out typos and rewrites her thoughts. She signs the letters in careful script with a blue ballpoint pen. The correspondence contained in *Letters to Goya* is perhaps most emblematic of Jim's ability to channel the peculiarities of the human experience. The pages are full of little jokes, details both intimate and mundane. Through these pages the Duchess paints an entire universe of small-town life, while slipping effortlessly from 18th century Spain to mid-century west Texas.

The origin of the Duchess in Jim's story is a drawing lifted off the back of a bathroom wall, a simple pencil sketch that in the roughest of ways calls to mind Goya's alleged portrait of the Duchess of Alba, *The Nude Maja*. Though disputed by recent scholarship, for centuries the relationship between Goya and his young widowed patron, the Duchess of Alba, was the source of speculation and often spoken about as one of the great romances in Spanish history. Goya did portraits of the young duchess and her husband, whom she married when she was only 13 years old. The duchess was beautiful and eccentric. In one of her earliest encounters with the painter she arrived at his studio and asked him to apply her makeup, about which Goya wrote to a friend, "That is certainly more of a pleasure than painting on canvas!" (Hagen, Rose-Marie and Rainer Hagen. *Goya*. Taschen, 2016, page 41.) When the duke died in 1739, the young duchess was only thirty-four years old. In the months following the death of her husband, the duchess, then the wealthiest woman in Spain, retreated to the coastal town of Cádiz where she invited the fifty-year-old Goya to join her. In the months that followed, Goya would draw and paint the Duchess scores of times. The paintings showed the duchess as a sensual being, dressed often in clothes that signified her connection with the popular classes of her time, as well as Goya's devotion to her (such as "Solo Goya/Only Goya" traced in the sand at her feet). There is no historic evidence of a real-life romance between the impetuous duchess and the deaf, disabled and blind painter from a much lower class but the paintings themselves laid the background for centuries of rumor and speculation.

Magee's *Letters to Goya*, the first part of the book, were composed during a brief visit to Sweetwater, Texas, the home town of a co-worker from his days working on a Texas oil rig. Rather than call in on his friend unannounced, Jim instead went into the town's library and buried himself in days of microfiche from the town's local paper in 1955. Many of the details found in the Duchess' correspondence are lifted directly from these pages—Sears bathmats on sale for a dollar, a columnist's tips for becoming a gracious lady, Splash Day Weekend in Galveston, and the Yankees beating Baltimore six games straight. The Duchess shares Jim's ability to be simultaneously connected to the mundane and the divine: she lives an existence in which "every shred of life foretells the future," simultaneously seeing signs in the simplicity of the paper peeling off her wall and the grandeur of a vision of "Ezekiel galloping on a fiery dapple with flames coming from his mouth." In the Duchess' world, as in Jim's own, it seems quite natural that everyday life suddenly cracks open to expose something close to religious ecstasy: the Duchess beginning "to kiss everything in sight"—her arms, her feet, the chair she is sitting in, even the refrigerator door.

The second half of the book, *Titles*, is a selected compilation of Jim's titles, created over several decades, and often many years after the visual works they "title." Over the years, the titles have been both displayed alongside the work, and read aloud/ performed by the artist as a complementary practice, again finding their home in a middle place, something between spoken word poetry and performance art. Jim's titles function as independent works of dialogue and contemporary poetry which provide an evocative narrative for work that, visually speaking, is largely abstract and non-representational. Jim tells us his titles are always written well after the creation of the work itself, sometimes many years later. They suggest an archeology of works themselves intimating that the objects they are connected to may be relics of lost or faraway places that are somehow intimately familiar and just beyond our understanding.

Jim is never alone in these places he takes us to. I have counted more than 50 individuals that have been conjured up just in the titles included here. Among them, a bearded man called Hersch, Helen with her left leg swelling, Julie rubbing her face and not knowing why, Louie on his tractor forever smiling, Morley, barefooted and runny-nosed, an old woman in a white-framed house, the plumber's wife, five recruits, and Juan standing naked under an overpass. Jim tells us that these are real people, characters from his everyday life but they may as well be characters from your life or mine. We are invited to recognize these individuals through the smallest of gestures, through the tiny details of their lives—a single gladiola bulb carried gingerly in a basket of mulch, a rented room wallpapered in last week's sports section, cats that must be fed. We cannot help but notice the glory of the world around us, in all of its mundane detail.

Jim's words arise from deep within the human experience. These poems come from fields and highways, from desert landscapes and kitchen tables. But they also come from his first-hand knowledge of urban spaces and his history in the gay street life of 1980s New York from which he mines the ecstasy and despair of bodies communing with strangers in darkened rooms, "pants pulled down, ricocheting from wall to wall." His words never disconnect from the everyday, they embody radically challenging aspects of a life lived without compromise.

The poems speak of another kind of embodiment as well, the joy of language as we speak it aloud, language that thumps rhythmically against the chest, escapes from the mouth with a tangible beat or a sigh. Spoken aloud, it is a language that fills the body and moves the air and the energy between us. "Short worms, long worms, wiggly worms and night crawlers, I willful Believer in the Weaver of light, spin into a canopy of symphonies." The poems have the structure of liturgy or ritual. They are songs of brokenness spoken joyfully. It is clear the author is luxuriating not only in the everyday details but also in the experience of language itself.

Jim's life-long practice of exposing himself to both the brightest sunlight and the darkest corners the world has to offer is visible now in his 73-year-old body. Held aloft on prosthetic legs, compromised by illnesses, blue eyes looking out from the craggy hollows of his face—he has opened his physical self to let the universe in. Yes, The Hill way out in the wilderness of the desert, part land art, part secular temple, is the seminal work of his life. Yet, as you come to know Jim, you realize that The Hill in all its enormity is a mysterious collaboration of all the many voices he carries around in his heart and mind. And he does so with fierce determination. He wants to make sure that nothing is left undone.

Letters to Guyu—this complete book of Titles, letters, poems, or "miniature dramas" as Jim calls them—is a revelation of that collaboration. Annabel, the retired librarian from the upper Midwest, who paints with the wild religious abandon of Blake or Martín Ramirez, has generously gifted the image of *Chillicothe Lady* for the book's cover. Horace Mayfield, the reclusive gay painter with whom Jim shares a modest bungalow (aka "Pompeii") across from El Paso's notorious boot hill Concordia Cemetery, is a compassionate presence in the nooks and crannies of these words. And of course there is James Magee—the blue-eyed, wild-haired visionary, maker of The Hill and massive steel and glass assemblages—who has a great hunger for words. Like a medieval alchemist, he must transform what he sees and feels into language. The words come almost unbidden in the midst of his day. He speaks them aloud, and then he writes them down, receiving them from who knows where. If some day, you are very lucky, Jim will recite one or more of these titles to you in his big bardic Irish voice, raw and beautiful utterances, rooted to the earth yet transcendental, something close to prayers, breaking the silence and dancing through empty spaces like the wind itself.